The Fortunate Islands

Susan Kelly-DeWitt

MARICK PRESS

Library of Congress Cataloguing in Publication Data

Kelly-DeWitt, Susan
The Fortunate Islands.
Poems in English

ISBN: 978-0-9712676-6-4

Copyright © by Susan Kelly-DeWitt, 2007

Design and typesetting by Sean Tai
Cover design by Sean Tai

Cover image by Rafael Trelles; www.rafaeltrelles.com

Printed and bound in Canada

Marick Press
P.O. Box 36253
Grosse Pointe Farms
Michigan 48236
www.marickpress.com

Distributed by spdbooks.org

for David

Contents

I
CREDO

Question Mark Café / 3

Summer of the Grandmothers / 4

Francis in Ecstasy / 5

Nuptial / 6

The Fortune Teller / 7

The Trees / 9

Bypass / 11

Egrets at Bolinas Lagoon / 12

Your Sailor / 13

Credo / 14

II
WHISKEY NIGHTS

Whiskey Nights / 17

The Day Gandhi Died / 18

Corporal Blood / 20

My Father Wearing an Aloha Shirt, 1951 / 21

Bad Blood / 23

Paint-By-Numbers / 24

Pomegranates / 25

Sugar Water / 27

Migraine / 28

Mail Order Minister / 29

Waiting for Garcia / 30
Crossing the Mojave at Night / 31
His Grave / 32
Cold Sweat / 33
Country Ghost / 34
Why I Don't Like to Travel / 35

III

INVENTING ANNA

June Night / 39
Inventing Anna / 40
Odalisque / 41
Painting Class / 42
The Old Sacramento Cemetery / 44
Dope Cocktail / 46
San Francisco, 1949 / 48
Poem for a Woman Found Dead Along Interstate 5 / 51
Roller Derby / 52
Apparition / 53
Abandoned House / 54

IV

RED HILLS AND BONE

Fifty-One / 59
Salt / 60
The Snail / 61
Crows at Evening / 62
Prison Garden / 64

Storm Brewing / 65

Bales Along Highway 4 / 66

Redding Town / 67

Red Hills and Bone / 68

How Will My Soul Get Free / 70

V

THE FORTUNATE ISLANDS

Water Signs / 73

Egrets Along the Yolo Causeway / 74

Latch-Key Kid / 76

L. L. Bean Catalog / 78

Song for my Father / 79

Middle Mountains / 81

If You Want to Know / 83

To Van Gogh: A Confession / 85

Writing Class / 86

Amherst / 90

The Fortunate Islands / 92

Acknowledgements / 93

Ptolemy was free, however, to lay his prime meridian,
the zero-degree longitude line, wherever he liked.
He chose to run it through the Fortunate Islands...

— Dava Sobel, Longitude

I

Credo

QUESTION MARK CAFÉ

I've been sipping coffee in the dark café
which is my today-mind uncurtained: stark café.

The morning started crying for no apparent reason.
The dreads were circling, shark café.

How marooned I feel on this island of thought.
I'm reviving like a half-dead verb in the word café.

Name a word, any word. *Soul* could be the one you
choose. Go ahead, it's okay, in the last remarks café.

*Who if I cried would hear me among the angelic
orders?* (Rilke. The same old question mark café.)

Today I'm that torn moth lipping the jack-
in-the-pulpit of history, who'll fly away: ghost café.

SUMMER OF THE GRANDMOTHERS

They come back in their white
shifts, their ruffled shawls of salt
white, the way the dead always return
when you need them the most —

when it's too hot to do anything
but picture the worst — the Bomb
finally fallen, the world burned-up,
the entire planet radioactive —

when you are too weak to do anything
but lie in a stupor and call them back
to drift at your side, in eyelet dresses
of old starlight, fresh-faced and cold.

FRANCIS IN ECSTASY

Francis lifts his arms and the swallows
return to Capistrano, their brown heads
nodding haloes of feathery song.
He is standing outside himself
in an Italian version of *ekstasis*,
the bloody eyes of the stigmata
winking from his feet and callused palms.
Seeing him there, like a canticle of the sun,
who can tell the Inquisition is preparing
its medieval fresco, smoothing its wet lime
plaster walls; grinding up its artists'
bones into the pigments from which Bosch's
Garden of Earthly Delights will be born.

after Bellini

NUPTIAL

I recognize the look of dislocation
I wore in my early twenties.
The woman wearing it is in a hotel
room, sitting on the bed; alone
with her thoughts and her poppy
camisole. She has the comfort
of four silent walls, the nuptial
of solitude. Whatever (who-
ever) she left behind is painted
into the night sky outside – a ruin
of light in a parked sedan, pale
auras of streetlights, like a string
of Hail Mary's along the avenues.

THE FORTUNE TELLER

of course, it's Paris
she's come out into the winter

night to tell a future
and confirm

a past

to find the cards
at home in their houses —

serious business, a fortune
teller must eat

her hands rest on three
cards: a decision!

(the grain of the table
swirls, mysterious hard-
wood lake)

       une grotesque poudrée

she's no sunflower
in a field

of sunflowers — no
she is the blackest tulip
the sumptuous

glistening *Queen*
of the Night

how carelessly the cards
turn their backs.

after a photograph by Robert Doisneau

THE TREES

Who is to say
the trees aren't frightened too
waiting in the cold in the dark

keeping watch while the wind
stomps heavily up the invisible
stairs to the cells to the attics

of the leaves while the crawlers
and climbers and fliers crash
through their tangled heads

like nightmares while the white
hawk glides while the silver cockroach
of the moon slides over the black

sky-boards while the limbs creak
and the walls of the branches
groan full of stickpins and wings

full of bones and feathers
full of jaws and razor teeth
while the souls of the dead

creep back to their graves
in the jungles of the faraway
in the absolutes of belief

or superstition who is to say
they don't wake exhausted
before dawn having thrashed

having thrashed about all night
in their beds of earth in their twisted
sheets of snuffed starshine?

BYPASS

When they cracked open your chest, parting
the flesh at the sternum and sawing

right through your ribs, we'd been married
only five weeks. I had not yet kissed

into memory those places they raided
to save your life. I could only wait

outside, in the public lobby
of private nightmares

while they pried you apart, stopped
your heart's beating and iced you

down. For seven hours a machine
breathed for you, in and out. God...

seeing you naked in ICU minutes
after the surgery – your torso swabbed

a hideous antiseptic yellow
around a raw black ladder of stitches

and dried blood. Still unconscious,
you did the death rattle on the gurney.

"His body is trying to warm itself up,"
they explained, to comfort me.

EGRETS AT BOLINAS LAGOON

They looked like callas or tulips
you could gather with a fist

or white amaryllis
you could snip from their shimmering
place in the world

you could slip from their stems
with sharp scissors

but they were toiling
the salt under-veins, tunneling
the weedy caverns

with yellow pickaxes
hunting up
a shining nugget
of flesh.

I thought of Van Gogh again:
"Making progress is like miner's work."

The birds that glowed like headlamps
were transformed by those alchemical
words, into painters and poets.

That same night
I woke nauseous, in a sweat
with all the old worries.

YOUR SAILOR

tried to lick childhood
clean from my mouth, holding
me down on grandmother's cast
iron bed when no one was
looking, pinning me to the sheets
by my reedy nine-year old wrists
and French kissing
me (you never knew).

His sailor collar fell
forward like white wings
against his shaved head;
his tongue fluttered
in my mouth and took
my breath away.

Then you married
him, your first husband.
I took this as a sign:
You were the pure one.

CREDO

I believe

in the way a bee enters a Rose
of Sharon with its whole gold dollop
of a body, expecting to back out
again, into the dry daylight,

expecting to return
home to the hive of the busy
and living, loaded with the stuff
of honey.

I believe

in the night-crazed
boats of the crickets, their wavery
flotations of song, more steady
than my heart-
beat

in the deeper grasses
we call love —

I believe

in their fevered appetites,
their pithy sermons
on brevity.

II

Whiskey Nights

WHISKEY NIGHTS

He was still human
but he grew guttural and cruel.

Even asleep
he would thrash at us and howl
like a wounded animal.

What was it that tore
his insides?

Once he wrapped himself
in an electric blanket, plugged it in
and stretched out on the wet grass
"to watch the stars."

We prayed he would
electrocute himself.

(Dear God, those howls –)

Those were our moonless nights,
love at such low tide we felt death
was the only possible future.

When the priest offered
the blessing at his funeral, I saw
a light in the shape of a man rise
out of his coffin and walk
soberly toward me.

THE DAY GANDHI DIED

I was only a few weeks old —
continents away in the hilly city
where fog hung on until three,
at which time, like clockwork,
my mother walked me up Taylor
Street, in vague sunshine.

My grandmother had journeyed
overseas on the Matson Line
to help with my birth. Her diary
that evening, 1/30/48, reads:
Home all day again. The virus
flu has hit San Francisco
and the schools are closed.

No mention of Gandhi's death
in her blotchy blue-black script —
that day, or any other.

I was quiet, a "good baby."
My eyes were already fixed
and alert. They saw the important
things clearly: the woman reaching
down to lift my weight, the propped
bottle on the pillowcase,

the angry man (who was
my father) in the background —

distinct shapes, larger than life,
though they also belonged
to a world removed.

CORPORAL BLOOD
PORT MORESBY, NEW GUINEA, 1943

He poses for the cameraman-gunner,
who captures him now for the future,
for this moment when I look and look,
trying to see beneath his jungle face.

Soon he will have a heart
attack and survive. He will live
a few years after that, a double
blind life of sober days and whiskey
nights; mornings he will vomit pure
blood, and it will seem to those who love him
that some invisible shrapnel festers his soul.

Then the burst of darkness, the flare
of blank exploding behind his eyes
will signal Death's Spartan troops.
He cannot see them now, as they march
through the door of a hospital
continents away; for now

he sways in the myth of victory,
a young liberator on foreign soil.

MY FATHER WEARING AN ALOHA SHIRT, 1951

Orchids straddle his back,
clamber over his chest
pocket, wind his belly,
his shirtsleeves, his stink
of whiskey and sweat.

Vodka and thirst
thirst and vodka
which comes first

Orchids
with little grass huts
and hula dancers.

And he's wearing
a *lauhala* hat
for the heat
on his head.

His shadow floats on the sand
like a shiftless angel

His throat is bare —
the thirsty place is bare,
is tan and open
to the *mauka* breezes.

Relaxed and open,
the unbuttoned collar,
the dry whiskey pipe.

Posing, an old
kamaaina – near the Hala
tree at Kuhio Beach –

near the magic healing
stones which will never
heal him.

The light will be drawn out
of his bones in their flower

He can't see
into the sun, the direct
glare of his future:

Death is formal,
buttons the eyes too tight.

BAD BLOOD

What did I know – a child of four
with sluggish bones, rickety
blood?

I dutifully swallowed
the ugly pills they handed me.

I hadn't yet understood
that the entire house
had bad blood,

needed a spiritual vitamin –
love a mineral
lack.

Even the houseplants
grew spindly and thin,
struggling for light

in that anemic life –
only the angers
grew fat.

PAINT-BY-NUMBERS

Colors belonged to God
but to make a world
I could borrow eight.

The expensive "thirty-two
jewel tone enamels"
belonged to rich girls

with backyard swing sets
and fathers
who would never drink

Vitalis strained through Wonder
Bread martinis.

POMEGRANATES

My mother, gray bird
beside a white bowl
of pomegranates.

They flare
        against her face,
creating an odd
                        balance.

She is retelling the family
myths. In this one, her mouth
is cut and bleeding, her teeth
pop out like seeds.

It is winter.
My father is King
of the Underworld.

"My whole mouth,"
she explains, drawing open
her lower lip, exposing the hidden
scars, "was pulp."

I memorize exactly, word
for word:

*He was quick
and strong, his punch
like a boxer's.*

We'd been married
only six months, still newlyweds...

as I pluck a pomegranate
from the bowl, hack it

open, place

a single blood
red seed on my tongue.

SUGAR-WATER

Fake grenadine in the plastic trumpet
flower feeder, slung from a crabapple's stub.
Our hummer arrives on schedule – dives
at the suck holes fringed in yellow petals –
stabs a quick nip.

> Throat-flash
> lit ruby as
> a wino's cheeks.

I am telling you our father's story, easing you
into it, censoring the parts about probation
violations, driving drunk, arrests. So peaceful
a scene for his sobering history. I can't help
wanting to sugar it for you.

Soon I may recite, as if you were a child again,
the tale of the drunkard who died so miserably,
the gods took pity and allowed him to be reborn
as a hummingbird, called forth by what is sweet.

MIGRAINE

The soul exists
but it is smaller than we think
particles of scattered
light fused

to the size of a
bee. I know this
because I saw
the soul last night.

Soul, I said, It's you —
and it drew near
and it hovered like a worker
and it changed colors
rose, to violet, to yellow
as if to signal, *Yes* —

I felt heat and stillness
something electric
from a swollen vein

at the center
of my being
and an inner eye
bled open.

MAIL ORDER MINISTER

Under his gabardine suit,
under the pack of Camels
and the Paper Mate pen,

stuck inside
the pocket of the Fruit
of the Loom undershirt,

the business card said,
"Minister: Doctor of Divinity,
Divine Life Church."

I had never known my father
to do anything
but laugh at the idea

of religion.
He had a premonition,
someone said after —

and the comfort of believing
he finally held the key
to something —

heaven, maybe.

WAITING FOR GARCIA

Guys are yelling in their holding cages
while they wait for transfer to The Hole.

The cages are steel mesh, half the size
of phone booths. They're wedged

inside like Supermen, without a change
of clothes. Troublemakers. It's noon.

It's cold. I just want to record the day:
January 2, 1995. One guy is rapping.

All I can make out is "burn, butt, slut."
We're waiting for a guard named Garcia.

How not to see him as God-like when he comes,
with boots, billy club, handcuffs, gun?

CROSSING THE MOJAVE AT NIGHT

This is how we outran
the word *Fugitive:*

The needle climbed
the glowing dial of digits,

the tires lifted off
to become night air

as my father topped
ninety.

The warrant
at his back scratched

its head, flashed
its bloody reds

and began the slow
wail that followed us

across three states.
The swollen vein

at his temple grew
tough as pipeweed.

HIS GRAVE

He's perfected here; zipped up
in his moist pocket of cemetery
dirt; the brassy flag of the dead

planted snugly above to claim
his clavicles' bony epaulets
for the infantry of devouring angels,

the two sunken cups stuffed
with slumped chrysanthemums
and carnations I've brought

as bouquets. Poor flowers!
They don't even know enough
to stand at attention: shoulders

back, feet together, spine straight.
They hunch like me, bowing
with a gesture of willows. *How*

has my river run so swiftly by?
(Each bloom on its spindle spills
out of its cup, falls down, tumbles

forward like a drunk into my squat
shadow.) They refuse to sway here
gaily, to liven things up.

COLD SWEAT

Last night
I woke up
cold, in bed
next to you.

The hair
at the nape
of my neck
was wet.

Perhaps
my spirit
was weeping
into my pillow.

Perhaps
my father,
dead now
twenty

years,
came sailing
down the river
one last time

and I ran
to greet him
through the wet
grasses.

COUNTRY GHOST

Here he is, sweat
on his forehead

and on the white collars
of callas tucked
among proficient weeds.

His debauchery
has gone to seed.

His young man looks
are evident again.

It's late to be out working
in this wind, but that's just
what he's doing, spading

and planting
the good.

The scent of star jasmine bleeds
its Chanel into the wide
warm breeze.

He looks refreshed
after his thirty years sleep.

WHY I DON'T LIKE TO TRAVEL

They loaded us
into the car – a blue
Pontiac. Father
hid the shotgun, shells
in the trunk; mother
brought along a few
pictures, our clothes.

I have forgotten
what I carried, except
for the small hand
of my brother.

We locked the door
to the tract house.
We said goodbye
to the sweet alyssum
mother had planted.

We left before daylight
and drove through the desert
across the state line.

My father must have thought:
Now I'm safe.

My mother must have worried:
What happens next?

I looked out the window
as the sun came up,
gentle then harsh
in the east.

III

Inventing Anna

JUNE NIGHT

The moon dipping its fingers in ink.
Darkness sucking a star's hot thumb.

The sentience at the heart
of the universe seems palpable:

A storm of gardenias rocking and moaning.
A white rose's perfumed croon of snow.

The murmur, murmur, murmur
of alyssum, honey sweet —

as though night had been given over
to a crowd of wild girls

camped out on humid bed rolls
of jasmine.

INVENTING ANNA

This morning Anna's hummingbird lights
the pollen wicks, the burnt orange
lanterns of Chinese maple

as another day begins in the short series called
June, July and August, and each blossom shakes
out the night's wet mix

of stars and dark. It is then that I imagine
a taciturn settler's lonely child-wife falling
into flattery or love

with the itinerant naturalist who named this
handful of darting plush, after that first
heated blush of arousal

at the girl's throat, then picked up again
for the East and anonymity.
Yes, my Anna will be lost

to oblivion and childbed fever three years
later, but the lover striking out across the plains
to meet his luck

will never quite silence those pliant white bells
of her petticoats ringing loose.

ODALISQUE

He thinks of her as still
life, a celadon bowl filled with ripe

colors, not some mythic female
balancing

a sky, though she was vast
at first, clotted with monumental

blues, and his eyes passed over her
like clouds.

So he's given her a hint of cantaloupe
chin, a grin of shadow

like a joke; he's stroked her
underarm stems in starkly,

boldly. Maybe tomorrow
he'll pose pears, a tilted

harem of them, but she'll be
free: vanished

except for this flesh-
trace she's left

like dense pollen
under his brush.

PAINTING CLASS

Deborah is a bee this morning: she stings
her boy Luther with the hard, flat back
of her hand. She pounds the table

twice with a crossboned fist, flashes
a tattooed wrist knotted with inky
lassoes. Nairobi is not going

to have any of it. She pounds
the table back – harder – hurls
four-letter words like live bait.

She is boldly beautiful in a cobalt
pique sundress that bares
a puckered constellation of scars

across her arms and chest.
(Her face is untouched except
where the kerosene lit

a pink ragged moon onto one
shined cheek.) She'd like to peel
off the crosshatched lizard skin

and fold it away, permanently
creased. Misty Lavender is mute
since her rape. She gets shaky

and afraid whenever Deborah
and Nairobi start to fight. Today
she crayons a purple scallop

of cloud in a choppy lemon
sky, and dangles a neon zigzag
cord from it – a rescue

helicopter's waxy rope
but no rescuer to slide down
with hope-burned palms.

THE OLD SACRAMENTO CEMETERY

Even the rows of stones
are askew, and on the unkempt
plots, nothing but bare
soil – a poor ceiling
for the women knitted together
under ghostly quilts
of leaf shadow.

Women who stitched
gingham, patched poplin, washed denim.
Women who liked things neat –
who planted roses, brought burlapped
from the East in Conestogas;

who put down roots
like submerged wishes.
Women who followed
the dreams of men West.

– The small pioneers went
first, feverish and nailed
into their wagons: *Sweet
Nettie*, whose bird-bones nest
among ivory sashes
a hundred years old.

And *Frankie*, buried in whalebone
cufflinks – scrimshaw fossils
of clipper ships with puffed sails.

Tintypes glint – tarnished
illuminations of souls
fixed under constellations
strange to them as western trees.

Under elm-tinted light, unlaced
leaves, what skeletal shadows
congeal over the graves of child
brides? – girl mothers who miscarried
and those other green girls

who still carry
the tapered fish-like traces
of infants curled
in the bone pods.

DOPE COCKTAIL

I wait uncrated
like an apple in a bin.
My mother

hunger grows
thin as I suck
my rosy knuckles

dry. Three days
unsorted I lie,
the other babies' cries

my only lullaby.
My poor mother's
plucked clean.

She sleeps
like the bitten,
as though a widow

spidered on
and clung
to anesthesia's nipple.

Her painless doze
is ether's snooze
gone haywire.

Even maternity
refuses to wake her.
My screams, however

shrill, can't snap
her back.
I'm assigned

but unclaimed.
I'm tagged, swabbed,
swathed unnamed.

No one of my own
blood touches me.

SAN FRANCISCO, 1949

We had no garden,
just a rooftop, tar
paper lawn, smokestack
shrubberies, chimney
flowers. Every day

you walked me,
up Taylor Street
to the drugstore,
the druggist who flirted
harmlessly.

Every day
you dressed us up
and walked me.

Every day you put on
lipstick, made yourself up
"to save your sanity."

Sometimes I wore
a ruffled bonnet.
You wore a purple hat,
purple shoes, splurged
on a violet bouquet.

That same year,
afraid, you held

a pillow over my face
to quiet me.

"Fear
is a terrible thing,"
you remind me.

How alone
you were in that city –
three thousands miles
from home, with your new
baby. No one
knew the man
who loved you
hated you,
struck you.

You wore
your exotic beauty
like a perfume.

Twelve years later,
I walked you.

Up the hallway
from the bathroom,
where death flirted,
lethargically.

Every few minutes
I walked you.

You wore no lipstick.
I dressed you
in your bathrobe
and walked you.

That same year,
ashamed, you held
a pillow over your face
to quiet me.

"Fear
is a terrible thing,"
I remind you.

POEM FOR A WOMAN FOUND DEAD ALONG INTERSTATE 5

She wears the same thin nightgown
over her soul that we do, the same poor
blood. For two hours the traffic rushes past

her body face down in the weeds,
her fingers hooked in the diamonds
of a cyclone fence, as if in death

she could pull herself up and walk away.
For two hours the commuters speed past
her underpants pulled down around her thighs –

some are shaving, listening to radio talk
shows, putting on lipstick, speaking into phones.
Underneath her torso feathery silver

poppy leaves push up through gravel,
called forth by the great cycles. Birds
of the fields rise over her, singing

again. Somewhere someone dear –
a mother, a sister, a lover, a friend – is waking
to her absence, is calling her by name

while her puzzled ghost, still wearing
its unfamiliar posture, its veil of brutal
perfume, is drifting slowly through

the cyclone's unlatched gate.

ROLLER DERBY, 1958

The sound of the rollers, grunts
and gasps; cartilage squinched
under padded knees. An elbow
to ribs, a shoulder to mid-torso
and Weston glided free of the pack

– hands to hips, wrists bent, ankles
flexed, as the referee blew the whistle.
Behind her the others collided, groaned
and toppled in a sorry pile of muscled
pectorals, satin shorts, bone and gristle.

I had never seen such unabashed
toughness in women. Buttressed
against pain, my women were docile,
genteel – their voices like silk
bandages over the wound of talk.

for Joan Weston, in memory

APPARITION

The tense apparition
of your neighbor, mowing
her lawn at midnight

under a streetlamp's fluorescent
moon; how the light curled
in waxy shavings

around her fierce, haggard
face, as if some sleepless
giant was being whittled
down to size.

ABANDONED HOUSE

the kind of house a child
passes, quick-step

regular unpainted
sorrow could live here

or loneliness wearing its sack
of old dresses

>   *something or someone sucked the night in*
>   *and held that breath*

inside a woman butters toast
the slices float
between her fingers

then the moon snaps her
up, up

through the roof beams
through a crack in the shingles

ha!

where's home now?

her ribs lift
over her face
her breasts

turn inside out like
pillowcases

IV

Red Hills and Bone

FIFTY-ONE

This morning when I searched the mirror
I found someone so vastly unfamiliar
that I recognized myself

as that other who has passed
her whole life inside my body,
the one who set up house

like a small, worried spider
at my birth. I found traces of her
torn webs under my eyes,

her busy scratchings at the corners
of my mouth. Later, when I sipped
my coffee from a warm mug,

I knew I tasted the full bitter flavor
with her lips, her tongue.

SALT

People still die for it.
            Gandhi marched to the sea
            for it. The heart spasms

            without it, the muscles
cramp. Last night I sobbed crazily
and the salt appeared on cue,

residue of fifty years.
            The body floats in it.
            The oceans are drenched in it.

            So,
the soul must feel
at home in it,

among the measuring
            spoons and shakers,
            among the bitter, shining

            crystals of salt —
even in the Great Salt
Desert. Boil

any pot of water
            and all your plans will vanish
            except for the salts.

THE SNAIL

I watch his narcotic plodding
across the Great Web of Being
or this one radial of it

which happens to be my slate
walk coming alive to morning
sunlight. Last night I spent

hours staring into the agate wells
which were the eyes of the old
and sick, as if they were spirals

whirling at the center of the Great
Void. (If you've been there you know
many cried out in their fright

and helplessness.) I was gripped
by a spiritual paralysis. Then
I came home again. I plodded

up this very path, past the beds
of flaring cosmos where the snail
is just now headed with his urges

intact. It was late and I slept
badly, while the Sturgeon Moon bled
a luminescent trail across the river.

CROWS AT EVENING

Twilights I see them
    thick as brambles
        of wild grape,

           a black smoke of them, a coil
        of black wires, a royal black
highway paved with feathers.

The light that has been bubbling –
boiling and singing!
in the yellow veins

        of leaves, in the muslin tongues
           of lilies, quiets
               to a muffled

           whisper, a slow
        rose simmer. The treetops
    color like tea stains

against the sky's zodiac
cup, as they pour, a torrent
of oil, as they funnel

        west out of sight;
           a Houdini of crows
           disappearing

             — recalled
        like some genie
    into a secret lamp,

into the day's interior
darkness.

PRISON GARDEN

Two guards with metal detectors search
for homemade knives in the formal rose garden

where inmates who have earned the privilege
can sit and admire the simple sky, a horizon

of scented blossoms in season (even thorns provide
a soul with its native weather) and a sculpture

built from manacles and prison rock. The guards are
vigilant, the inmates ingenious: they'll craft

weapons from twist ties, paper clips, even melted plastic
garbage bags; last year someone was killed by

a newspaper spear. There is also agapanthus here –
gazania, zauschneria, ceanothus, drought

tolerant xeric plants. They'll never have to pray:
Lord, how I thirst in this dry place.

STORM BREWING

Rags and rages,
rips and rapids, woolpacks,
heaps, sheets.

Dry leaves rise in whirlwinds,
twisters of twigs and dust.

Dust devils squirm the tilled fields,
churning feathers, grasses, pollens.

The sky is a thief, mutters the farmer.

All along the river the cottonwoods
shake and shake.

The moon squats like a cold white Buddha
above the exosphere.

There doesn't seem to be a *nirvana* anywhere.

BALES ALONG HIGHWAY 4

Stacked against the horizon of storm
clouds, they looked historical –
the field's bound feet.

We imagined we heard each of them
say, "We can't breathe
in these corsets. Undo us."

We couldn't resist the idea
of tinder in the eyes
of some twisted beholder,
his three bad wishes.

And after that a fire
could be heard in our minds
over the timid ears of corn,
the lowing of frightened cattle.

We thought of the match
and the machete.

We remembered Millet's
radical pastorals, his bent peasants
with their pitchforks and scythes, and short
harsh lives given up to labor.

We pictured the fragrant lion-
colored bales of hay
lying down with the fat
winter lambs.

REDDING TOWN

On Cypress Avenue I watch for the ghosts
of Wintu women with willow root baskets, pine nut
skirts, poles spread with the silver skins
and carmine flesh of drying salmon.

I spot them in a half-circle
along Churn Creek Road,
near a boarded-up deli.

They are watching a great-great-
granddaughter ($\frac{1}{16}$ on her father's side)
pump unleaded into her battered pickup,
a sleek feather dangling – the power
of Eagle – from her rearview.

I wonder if their baskets still hold blackbird
feathers, salmon bones, a future.

RED HILLS AND BONE

In the Lotus Garden Restaurant,
a man overturns the cluttered table
for six where his family is gathered.
He grabs the lip

of the table and flips it quickly, like
a child flips a bug, so the underbelly
of rough pine appears but the napkins
vanish, so the tablecloth's

lilies clamp their petals and the scooped
China moons, heaped with noodles and exquisite
fish, swim to the floor, so the chopsticks
un-X themselves from the thick

dragon plates and the glassware shatters,
so the tea in its rice-seed cups spatters
jasmine over the stunned waiter's shoes.
This is the precise moment —

as the man's face pulses with sudden
rage; as the throng in the restaurant
swivels its many faces burning in unison
toward them, one blank questioning

sun; as the waiters in their spotless
white aprons begin to flutter and circle
like scavenging gulls — this is exactly
the moment when the family climbs

68

the blood red hills, determined
to disappear into them, to leave no trace –
erasing themselves like soft wood chips
into fire; leaving the fury of the man

far behind; leaving him alone
to inhabit his desert
skull's wildness
like a vestigial bone.

abstracted from a painting by Georgia O'Keeffe

HOW WILL MY SOUL GET FREE

Will she burst through my body
like a showgirl in a cake? Will she coil

like blue smoke from my fontanel?
Will she pry herself loose through my clamped

teeth? Will she yank herself out
like a sword by my hilt, or will she steam

out through the pores of my skin? Will she tug
herself out, on a hook through my gut, or leak

like a thread of pale urine? Will I scratch her
like a flea from my left ear? Will my lungs

cough her out, wet clot of soul?
When that time finally arrives, how

will my transparent twin escape?
Will something I can't recognize or name,

some undetected power scatter her
fragrant powders to the four far corners,

or will she drift like a torn veil of atoms
and dust? Tell me, will she zigzag

like some erratic anti-moth
toward a secret corolla?

V

The Fortunate Islands

WATER SIGNS

In the book I am reading, Lord
Byron is still alive but Shelley
has just drowned. The chill tons
close over him like the Whale
God's jaws. A few plain words
across one page, and he is gone.
The great icy lid slams shut
over his troubled shining.

It is July 8, 1822.
In ten days his body will beach
with the sopped volume of Keats'
poems open inside his coat pocket.

I have put the book aside
before news of the poet's death
can spread. It lies on its back
on the bare floor, its broken spine
becalmed, in a quiet lake of sunlight.

EGRETS ALONG THE YOLO CAUSEWAY

Every day I watch how they float
into the wind; how they stretch
their legs out behind them

like burnt matchsticks,
then fall, heavy as drugged
eyelids into muddy browns, crushed

iris blues; how they plunge
suddenly as danger
or stupor into the shadows

of a ditch. Often, climbing up
out of a shadowed place myself —
out of a muggy airless wetland

where thoughts grow dark
seeds like wild rice — I spot one,
a loner, drifting below the causeway,

wading the weedy edges of slough
grass, his yellow beak gleaming
like a cutlass. Focused

on the task at hand: Beauty
is not even a vague
idea to him, or truth. He'll stab

whatever helps him
live. Every day as I travel past them
from the prison where I teach

men to uncage hope, snap
open the hinges, I watch how they lift
from the rich delta plowlands,

how they glide free – a wholeness –
like one white feather, unlocked from its body,
shiftless and holy.

LATCH-KEY KID

At the Japanese School
I sat at the rear
with my friend Sharon Kido.

Sensei konichiwa —
I bowed with the others
when the teacher appeared.

When I stood I put my weight
on the outside edges of my feet,
to walk bowlegged like Sharon
whose parents were born in Nagasaki.

The classroom then
boxes of rice candies, Botan,
male for Peony, crinkled inner
wrappings that dissolved
on the tongue, a tiny prize
inside, then salty packages
of cracked seed, dried squid.

(Ten years after my mother's friend
Ozzie disappeared into the Pacific,
after Pearl Harbor, the fury,
the bombers flying in over the Pali,
here we were.

I idolized Sharon, absorbed
the way her family left their shoes

behind on the *lauhala* mat and
stepped cleanly into the house.)

Japanese School then home
to our empty studio apartment –
the shared garden bursting
with cannas and ginger,
the strayed bullets still buried there
that we liked to dig up and keep
like dull brass seeds in jars –
until my mother came home
with my baby brother, from her
job at Hickam Air Force Base.

L. L. BEAN CATALOG

The clock on the back cover,
"Big Ben, Moon Beam,"
is stopped at ten after ten

in "blue periwinkle," that flower
we named to conjure
a color for my father's eyes.

His ticker stopped thirty-
five years ago, the old black
telephone rang the alarm,

the "gently illuminating light"
would not wake him, nor
the bell sound. Sometimes

I dream his hands are holding
more than hours and minutes.
Still, I hope he's found good

sleep in Sunflower Bedding,
under a Compass Quilt.
I believe his is a permanent

snooze feature, but just in case
he does awake, let it be
a hopeful rise and shine.

SONG FOR MY FATHER
BURIED NEAR THE FEATHER RIVER

He is still
awake
down there,

waiting
for the first
breath

of storm to puff
his lugsail,
his hands

folded stiffly
as a last
bitter

wind
over his tight
chest. Lightly

the Feather
River will rise,
singing

its dark song,
skull song
of uprooted

trees, bursting
like a swollen
vein into

the peach
orchards; splitting
bone, burl

seed
and branches;
swelling

to lift
his cumbersome skiff
into the open sea.

MIDDLE MOUNTAINS

1.

I was hiking the Middle Mountains,
the Histum Yani, where the Great Spirit
dropped some leftover dust
from the creation. It was a stormy
day, the mountains as blurred
as a late Monet, huge clouds like gray
water lilies lashed to each other
by icy winds and driving rain.
My father's grave was a few miles
to the east; his bones corralled
like the settlers we passed in the fenced
plot – the one-legged rancher who outlived
three wives (each of them dead before
thirty-five) buried with him –
on a hilltop with blue oaks.

2.

At the Palace of the Legion
of Honor in San Francisco,
you can stand at the far end
of one long wing and see through
a series of portals, into and past
the crowded galleries, to the famous
water lilies, the blur of pink blooms
floating on the far wall, the artist's

diminished sight still blossoming
in a bright square of museum light.

So it was that I found myself
at the entrance to an old barn —
among rat droppings and old farm
machinery, among abandoned spider-
weavings, within sight of an old Maidu
grinding stone pocked and pooled
with rainwater — staring through the portals
of memory, unearthing the old bones
of a young bride — myself — who floated
once in someone's arms, pink, fleshed,
out of focus in another life.

3.

Love has many graves
covered over in haste
by the side of the road —
victims of the overland journey.

The wolves of memory
will rip them open, feed on what lived
once, and vanish again.

IF YOU WANT TO KNOW

... the understanding is more vision than it is watchfulness ...
  — Eudora Welty

You must go back four hundred years
to Giovanna Garzoni's *Plate of White
Beans*; you must open a pod, slide one
fingernail in along a puckered seam.

You must speak of the six plump
beans that pop out like fat embryos,
of how any shallow dish is worn
along the gleam, the glaze uneven;

how the leaves tucked in around
the mounded beans are mangled;
how the foreground is stippled
(a *Garzoni technique* — she who

painted a Holy Family before she was
sixteen; who never married but had
formidable patrons; who traveled to Venice,
Naples, Florence, Rome, where

she settled, 1654, as an old artist-
spinster; who willed "a considerable
sum of money and all her possessions"
to the Academy of Saint Luke, and so

had her monument erected in the church
of Santi Luca e Martina thirty years
after her death), a homely cloth,
a mottled Naugahyde, texture of potato

skin. You must read the wallpaper
ghosts of the white carnations rising
behind the subject, the brown tasseled
pedicels, dried sepals that seem to gasp,

probe, toil – that grope and hunger
like foraging sea snails – even
the casual red carnation in one corner
of the composition – as a survival

text. But do not write *Vanitas*, or that
the flowers mean decay – not here, not
in this poem. You must imagine the two
white carnations as spirits, children

she would have had, twin palindromes;
that the red one tossed down so casually
spells out with tempera the name of her
equal, her vivid love.

TO VAN GOGH: A CONFESSION

I too might have despised you –
found you smelly, uncouth
and your paintings garish.

I might have passed you by
on a country road and laughed
at your raveled straw hat,

your ravenous eyes.
I might have joked with the others
about the crazy, the lunatic

colors – wild sunflower
yellows, petals dripping
like wax from your ignited

fingers. I might barely have noticed
your carefully arranged
patience, the paint box

on fire, you like an écorché
in a corner of landscape
at the edge of a saffron field.

WRITING CLASS

Joseph presents me
with a small arrangement:
French marigolds, Shasta
daisies, pansies – which
I put into water
in a Dixie cup.

Rule Number One: *No*
picking flowers.

Zinnias, agapanthus,
black-eyed Susans –
corymbs, cymes, disks;
heliotrope, belladonna –
filaments, rays, rosettes

in full summer flower
along the edges of the prison
yard, all along the visitor's walkway
but this nosegay
is petty theft.

———

Larry writes
twenty-four lines, exactly
the number required
for a prison poetry contest.

I love him. Nothing romantic —
I mean, he has my respect.

He works in chopping
cotton at five, a poem in five
voices; the quiet one
is little Larry's — the other
four grownups shout.

"Forgive,"

he writes at the bottom
margin (he feels
bad for me — I have to read
his poem and he can't
spell).

———

First Lesson:
Watch your back —

so Richie
tells me. (He bloodied
his head on his cell
wall, trying to catch
a glimpse of wild
turkeys in the Yard.)

Second Lesson:
Wonder is alive,
even here.

Write a poem called
"The Two-Sided Man"
I tell them. I begin
to write my own —

it starts: *A quilter*
could have a field
day with this: Hounds-
tooth, Jericho cloth…
(who knows why
it begins this way.)

I get stuck on how
the trumpet keeps sounding,
how the walls keep
not-falling down.

———

Here are a few lines written
by inmates number CL860,
HK139, NG641 and KT855
(these numbers are invented,
to protect the real):

> *The wood is screaming.*
> *Magical poems.*

> *I am so tired, maliciousness*
> *of growing old.*

Time clawing.
Yellow river.

Fueled by memory
of what is yet to be.

AMHERST

I am breathing east of the past, closed hours, locked doors
plumerias, a postcard of old ocean

I scribble my mother's name into a spiral notebook
She forgot consolation, thumped us on the back
like consumptives

The mornings revived us (we subtracted the nights)
Mother crowded out her disappointment with pancakes, fried
egg sandwiches wrapped in waxed paper

At this my grandfather scoffed, his son who never was
pinched us on each cheek: Wake up!
He drank from a thermos of angers

The kitchen grew calm – a period piece
a pried open clam. A coffin sat on the table
a tongue beside the fresh squeezed orange juice

My brother erased the categories of joy from his blackboard
He chalked the moon into one corner
He was only an imp with polio in his veins

He charmed the night nurses
and kept my dreams awake all night

My grandfather had escaped both World Wars, too young
for one, too old for the other

He went to war with grandmother instead
She planted scissors in his left shoulder
He planted daughters in her, more daughters

My father kept bullets, a pistol, a shotgun
God spilled a cloud of raised eyebrows
the day he was born

Mother refused to stay put between the eyes
The kitchen filled with tombstones

In a cupboard, my father's bronze Oak Leaf Cluster
his jars of salted pig's knuckles
We swallowed carefully among the ghosts

I found a book with Dickinson's poems
The room grew calm, a pried open clam
A coffin sat on the table

The sleigh bed, the dresser, there
she was, the white dress, the blue shawl
I could alter them, she said.

THE FORTUNATE ISLANDS

Here

each red maple leaf
five fingers begging alms

even the crescent moon
slicing a cloud

is a fortunate island
through which I draw

my prime meridian
my zero-line

In the ink-dark temple
the past seems far away

I can cross the wooden bridge
in either direction

(after *Maple Leaves at Mt. Takao, Kyoto*
by Komai Ki, 1747–1797)

Acknowledgments

Thanks to the publications where these poems first appeared, sometimes in earlier versions:

Americas Review: "Writing Class"
Bakunin: "Your Sailor"
Clockwatch Review: "Corporal Blood" (as "Photograph: Port Moresby, New Guinea, 1943")
Comstock Review: "My Father Wearing an Aloha Shirt, 1952"
Ekphrasis: "Abandoned House" (As "Cultivation and Neglect")
Hawaii Review: "Pomegranates," "The Old Sacramento City Cemetery"
Montserrat Review: "The Fortune Teller," "Bypass," "Sugar Water," "Crows at Evening"
North American Review: "To Van Gogh: A Confession"
One(Dog)Press: "Salt"
Poetry Southeast: "Nuptial"
ReDactions: "The Fortunate Islands"
Spoon River Poetry Review: "Apparition"
Stone Drum: "Cold Sweat" and "Song For My Father"
Tule Review: "Why I Don't Like to Travel"
Weber Studies: "Egrets at Bolinas Lagoon"
Women's Studies Quarterly: "Roller Derby, 1958"

"Summer of the Grandmothers," "Francis in Ecstasy," "His Grave," "Odalisque," "Fifty-One" and "Water Signs" appeared in *Poetry*.

"Whiskey Nights," "June Night," "Dope Cocktail," "San Francisco, 1949" and "How Will My Soul Get Free" appeared in *Prairie Schooner*, University of Nebraska Press.

"Egrets Along the Yolo Causeway" was published in *Richer Lives*, Redwing Press, 1998. "The Old Sacramento Cemetery" was reprinted in *The Sacramento Anthology: 100 Poems*, Sacramento Metropolitan Arts Commission, 2001. "Salt" was included in *O Taste and See*, Bottom Dog Press, 2003. "Bypass" appeared in *Poet Healer*, Sutter Hospital Arts and Literature Program, 2004. "Bypass" was also featured on *The Writer's Almanac*, Minnesota Public Radio, 2006. A number of these poems were included in the following chapbooks: *A Camellia for Judy*, Frith Press; *Feather's Hand*, Swan Scythe Press; *To a Small Moth*, Poet's Corner Press; *Susan Kelly-DeWitt's Greatest Hits, 1983–2002*, Pudding House Publications; *The Book of Insects*, Spruce Street Press; *The Land*, Rattlesnake Press. "Latch-Key Kid" appeared in *Cassiopeia Above the Banyan Tree*, in an electronic chapbook as *Mudlark #33*, and in print chapbook from Rattlesnake Press.

My thanks to all of the above, and to Stanford University for a Wallace Stegner Fellowship. I am especially grateful to Sandra McPherson for her expert editorial help with this collection; to Dennis Schmitz, Gary Short, Catherine French, Kathleen Lynch, Hannah Stein, Mary Zeppa, and to my friends and colleagues who have offered support and encouragement over many years; and to Rafael Trelles for his marvelous cover art.